BUTTKICKERS
Twenty Ways to Leave Tobacco

10th Anniversary Edition

Joanna NicciTina Free

To Lesia —
With so much LOVE!
Joanna Nicci Tina Free

Copyright 2021 Joanna Free

Cataloguing-in-Publication Data

Buttkickers: twenty ways to leave tobacco /

Joanna NicciTina Free

p.cm.

Includes bibliographical references.

ISBN: 978-0-9840239-4-3 (ebook)

ISBN: 978-0-9840239-5-0 (paperback)

1. Smoking cessation. I. Title.

HV5740.C86 2021

616.86506-dc22

PREFACE

On 11-11-11, I wanted to do something I'd remember for the rest of my life, and with a smile. So I got up early. At 6am I was in front of the computer. I wanted to see if I could get out of my own way and write a first and very rough draft of a little book – one you could fit in a pocket - telling you twenty ways to leave tobacco, and to complete that very rough draft on that day. I told no one of the plan because I knew that, if I did, I'd sabotage myself. I barely even told myself. I snuck up on it just as I'd snuck up on my buttkicking (after many failed head-on attempts) and that had worked out.

By about 11pm on 11-11-11, that very rough draft was done. I put it and myself to bed. I was proud and grateful to have spent that day that way; grateful because I knew that once again, as with *Kick Butts Take Names* in 2009, something was writing through me and with me and helping to get that done; helping me keep my hands on the keyboard and get out of my own way to let it.

I slept hard that night, emptied out.

If I'd been wiser, I would've gotten up the next day and gone in search of an editor to help me polish it up and make it into something I'd be proud to share. But I wasn't as smart as I was diligent. I've always been more of a worker bee than a queen bee and I can also be an impatient and fearful worker bee who's sure that if I don't get something done right away, there's too much of a risk that it won't happen at all.

I was also on a tight and tiny budget when I wrote that draft on 11-11-11, and so determined to be thrifty and fast.

So many people can't afford the help they need to kick. I wanted – want - to do my part to level the playing field, to make buttkicking something that's available to everyone, as available as tobacco or nicotine, and a lot less costly. And also, as soon as possible.

I was afraid that if I complicated things too much, my book wouldn't get out to market. That meant I needed a cheap and cheerful publishing option.

So instead of looking for an editor, I read that very rough draft to a couple of friends, I cleaned up the typos I could find by myself, found what was then some free and eager uploading help at Amazon Kindle Direct Publishing, got one endorsement for the back of the book from my friend Patrick Snow and asked my friend Jackie to help do the cover. I had the book available for Christmas gift-giving in December of 2011, just one month later.

I was proud as hell of that timeline: *I got 'er done!* I ended that year feeling pretty self-satisfied and pleased with my efficiency.

Then, as any writer knows (or quickly learns), once a book is done, it's time to *truly* get the book out into the world. I couldn't figure out why it was so hard for me to do that. One day, however, when I agreed to do a reading for an event, I noticed how I felt about the content. It was embarrassing... I was embarrassed to call it my own.

Writing a book draft is a bit like making a baby. You never feel 100% ready when you're writing that draft - or deciding to become parents - but you push on, literally and figuratively.

What's different is that, when you birth a baby into the world, you don't expect it to get out there and stand on its own. You *know* it needs nurturing, care and attention. You say *Yes* to some things and *No* to others and the baby learns how to grow and thrive, to stick around and to stay out of traffic.

A draft - and then a book - needs care and attention, too. It, too, needs to get *Yeses* and *Nos*. It needs to be helped along. I didn't do that for my little draft or for my book. I just put it out there, bumbling and defenseless, pooping in its own pants. I was a shit book parent. I didn't nurture that little book any better than I nurtured myself most days.

The other thing I did was to go against all of my own teaching: I did it alone. I didn't 'take names.' There's a wise African proverb, ***If you want to go fast, go alone. If you want to go far, go together.***[1] Of course, right?

Writing, editing, and publishing a book about buttkicking alone? Idiotic. I knew better but didn't do better. I would never have been well enough to write a book about buttkicking if I hadn't been part of a tribe that helped me kick and stay free years ago. But apparently, I had to learn that lesson again and in a new way.

In 2019, I discovered a platform called Patreon[2]. Patreon provided a way to receive from some and to serve others. Each contribution and contributor has helped to keep this mission alive and me engaged in the work of each buttkicking day. They have faith - in me and in this mission - that helps to sustain mine so that I don't need to carry that faith and the mission alone. Some of these supporters I've never met, yet their faith in me persists, just as my faith in you persists. Faith isn't rational, my friend.

The support of this community, this village, also means that, this time, we have the village to help bring this draft into the world. We've found an editor who is also a former smoker, a fellow butt-kicker. Others are joining the launch squad and still others have contributed their support in proof-reading and other parts of the care and attention a little draft requires. All of these village people have said *Yes* to being a part of this, each in their own way, with their own strengths. And the only way they could say *Yes*, was for me to ask them the question, *Would you be willing to help?*

I share this with you, dear reader, to consider how *asking* could transform your life.

To everyone who said *Yes* to my awkward asks and to my dodgy draft, thank you, thank you, thank you.

Now, let the buttkicking begin.

Together.

INTRODUCTION

Are you willing to forget every single useless thing you've learned in the interest of remembering the truth of who you are?

If you're like most humans, you've come to believe a lot of useless ideas over the years.

You've also heard – and accepted – stories that you've told yourself and everyone else so many times that you've made them true between your own ears and maybe even in the world around you, whether you intended to or not.

Most people who use tobacco have bought into (literally) a whole pile of nonsense that's of no use to them whatsoever. Many of them want to be free of it at least some of the time; 60-70% admit they want to kick it, some desperately so. Many others mask their discomfort and desire for freedom with bravado, clutching or entitlement. They need to make a stand for something in this world; it may as well be their drug of choice.

Some have even bought into the idea that tobacco use truly benefits them; that it's their little helper. In the short-term, catch-as-catch-can world of 'just get through the day' - sure.

In the bigger picture, that story could not be further from the truth.

We are all comfort seeking beings. Even people who are 'into pain' will tell you they get a massive release of feel-good chemicals in their body when they do the pain-inducing things that stimulate that release.

Tobacco and nicotine do indeed provide comfort, though at a tremendous cost. We know this going in. Even I, lighting up at the age of 12, knew it wasn't good for me. We seldom stop to calculate that cost, however (you'll find a chapter in here on doing the math so you **can** stop and calculate).

Here, though, we're talking about something much greater than the monetary cost. Tobacco takes our attention, hijacks our creativity, numbs us up and dumbs us down. We fall into a just-get-through-the-day kind of consciousness, which is a bit like no consciousness at all.

You didn't take shape in this miraculous body you inhabit – it's like a palace, a wonderland - to just 'get through the day', day after day, puffing away, until the day you fall over dead.

Stop and contemplate that for a moment. Reflect on your amazing body – billions of cells, all moving together to form muscles and bones, blood and hormones, mind, intelligence, consciousness…. Surely there is more to this brilliance than 'just getting through' life.

Like most of us using tobacco, you've learned to settle.

You settle for sucking on a stick that you've lit on fire, or shoved in a pipe or paper and ignited, or pushed between your cheek and gums. And you perceive that daily practice as pleasure and enjoyment and relaxation and comfort. In doing so, you've forgotten how amazing, how creative you are. Nicotine is a powerful amnesiac.

We'd forgotten that our human body is not designed to run on smoke; it's designed to shun and repel it. But bodies learn to settle, too. Your body has adapted to this pattern of behavior, to this long-term, self-depriving relationship with tobacco and nicotine.

Smoking, vaping, dipping - it feels like self-indulging but it's truly self-depriving. It's an impoverished and impoverishing way of comforting, nurturing and rewarding ourselves. Tobacco use is one of the ways the poorest among us get and stay poorer in all forms of wealth, including health.

We need – we all need - ways to ground, self-regulate and nurture ourselves. New ways, new practices; ways to connect that feel safe and comforting; nontoxic ways.

The weird - and frankly, creepy - thing about tobacco is it feels safe and smooth. It's been chemically engineered that way. Unaltered tobacco is not smooth. The tobacco available on the market has been 'stepped on' – that's a term used in the street drug world for drugs that are 'dirty' – that have been heavily chemically altered. Tobacco used ceremonially, in sacred ways, in its raw, natural form, is not something you would sit and inhale all day. It's got a natural harshness that would protect you from that, the way cyanide is bitter or rotting food gives off noxious fumes. If you think about it, the whole idea of tobacco is just a bit bonkers. Don't believe me? Listen to Bob Newhart's

short sketch, "Introducing Tobacco to Civilization."[1]
Step away from the idea of 'safe and smooth' and just
think about what you're actually doing here.

The industry has altered and then filtered
tobacco, so it's masked as something smooth instead
of biting. It also has chemicals added to it - like
ammonia - that make it cross the blood-brain
barrier rapidly - like crack does - to give that imme-
diate hit we've come to depend on. That's one reason
we call it drug dependency. **We depend on this
toxin to give us something we've trained ourselves
to stop seeking elsewhere.** We get less and less
creative, resourceful and brave as we come to rely on
the drug for everything from mourning to cele-
bration.

Most tobacco and nicotine users, past and
present company included, chronically and
profoundly under-nurture ourselves. We do this, in
part, because we've been raised by people who
under-nurtured themselves and taught us to do the
same. We also do this because we perceive the nicotine or tobacco we're using as a form of nurturing.
It's been engineered, chemically and in its shape and
mouth feel, to hit the brain that way; to trick us. So
as we are poisoning ourselves, we are telling

ourselves that we are rewarding, comforting and nurturing ourselves.

This is just one of many reasons we feel like we're going to die or fail to thrive without it. It's the mommy we wished we'd had, the daddy we can count on, the pacifier, the biscuit, the cookies and the milk, the thumb, the playtime. It's our everything.

Many people tell me, *I can't stop. It's the only pleasure I still allow myself.* I feel such deep sadness whenever I hear this. I remember, too, how I'd said that myself when I'd kicked all the other drugs except nicotine. We cut ourselves off from everything else that could nurture, reward or comfort us, or never allowed or learned to access those other things to start with. Many of us were surrounded by smokers in our lives when we started.

I've met some buttkickers who started so early that they went directly from pacifiers and thumb sucking to lighting up. So we are challenged to learn, adopt, adapt to and embrace new ways of seeking and finding comfort as buttkicking adults. Fortunately we don't need to do that alone. Mutual support communities - like 12 Step Fellowships[2] - are a bit like reparenting classes for us grownups, and they're now widely available.

Many of us go to food as a default when we're kicking. It, too, feels rewarding, and is even more widely available than tobacco. Sugar is one of the things used in the tobacco curing process. Even vaping is chemically engineered to feel rewarding in this way; many of the flavors taste sweet, designed to appeal to our desire for sweetness in our mouths and in our lives. So, sugar and sweetness become things we miss and seek out when we kick.

We also default to fats and other savory foods, because they, too, taste and feel nurturing. A great many people continue to use tobacco and nicotine in other forms for fear that they will gain weight when they kick. That's a realistic concern because tobacco is also an appetite suppressant. It suppresses our appetite for many things, including nurturing.

You could almost hear it saying, like some abusive partner, *Choose me over them. You don't need them.* And eventually, *Choose me over yourself.*

If tobacco suddenly quadrupled in price, many of us would find the means to get it, even if we had to beg, borrow or steal. But buy ourselves a weekly massage to help our body purge toxins and adjust to the new normal of buttkicking? Or commit to counseling to sort out and clear the trauma that initiated and drives the addiction? Or invest in some other special something that would fulfill the desires we're numbing with tobacco? No. Most of us are too stingy with ourselves – or too broke - to even give ourselves a good community for healing, transformation, and mutual support.

Our under-nurturing is so pervasive that we don't want to indulge in other forms of nurturing. *A carton of cigarettes will last me a week*, one buttkicker said. *How long will that massage or counseling session last?*

Again, this is one of the reasons the poorest amongst us have gotten poorer, in health and in all forms of wealth. Toxins – like junk foods - are compelling, highly accessible and relatively cheap. The good stuff (most of it) is more costly and less accessible. This book – and you reading it - is one small step in us changing that long-standing trend.

This kicking process will completely and utterly transform our lives, if we let it. I believe that's the greatest gift of any addiction: it drives us to meaningful connection with kindred spirits. It opens us up: to ourselves, to each other, and to something bigger and infinitely more powerful than we are by ourselves. That's the blessing embedded in the challenge.

HOW TO USE THIS LITTLE BOOK

Most people I talk with about buttkicking tell me they get discouraged, overwhelmed, tired and angry. I did. You try to get free; some of us try and try. And try.

The thing is: most try just one or two tools or tricks at a time. If you're still using tobacco now, with all of the messages, constraints, supports and pressures around you to stop, you probably need more than one or two tools to secure your freedom, for good.

To be comfortably successful at buttkicking, it's best to bundle. Bundling means you choose and do several things together and at the same time to replace the dosing, the sucking and blowing you've been doing a hundred or more times a day.

You need tools to set yourself free. New tools, a new pack, and a better story.

This pack of twenty tips and tools is meant to awaken you; to jog your memory, your creativity, your resourcefulness and your backside. As you look at these, on the page or in your mind's eye, you can ask yourself: which one will I try today, just out of curiosity? Just to see what happens?

Play with these ideas. See if you can have some fun with them. They're here for you.

There are, of course, more than twenty ways to free yourself from this SOB (smoky old butt) that's been tying up your hands and stealing your lunch money. You could probably think of more than twenty ways yourself, especially if you put heads together with other buttkickers. You're very creative. Humans are; that's human nature. We are also forgetful, though. We forget what we're made of and we forget what we're about.

If you're not ready for this transformation - this freedom - just yet, let's just get you ready to get ready to get free (read that part again if you need to; it's important). I'm not here to tell you what to do, or what your timing should be, or to decide what's in your toolbox. That's all up to you and all the forces operating within and around you.

You'll do it your way.

Most of us, we're told, will take six to nine attempts to get free. Six to nine attempts: try, learn, try, learn, try, etc.… get free.

But that's without this book.

We're here together to stack the odds in your favor. A new pack of things to reach for, a new pack to run with, too. A pack of buttkickers beats a pack of butts, anytime.

So, ready or not, let's continue this journey you've already begun.

CONTENTS

1. Words Matter   1
2. Children and Animals   8
3. What's That in Your Mouth?   10
4. Drink Up   12
5. To Air is Human   14
6. Get Out of The Way   16
7. See it, Say it, Draw it, Share it, Do it   19
   (and let it do you)
8. Go Outside and Play   22
9. Eat a Vegetable. Eat a Bean   25
10. Laugh Your Butt Off   28
11. Look Crazy, Get Sane   30
12. Tap Yourself Free   33
13. Come Out, Come Out, Wherever   38
    You Are
14. No More Nice Dead People   41
15. Do the Math   45
16. Better Living through Better   48
    Chemistry (or To Nicotine or Not to
    Nicotine)
17. Question Authority   53
18. Break – or Make – the Trance   59
19. The Grand Adventure   62
20. Kick Butts, Take Names   67

In Summary   73
Acknowledgments   81
Notes   85
About the Author   87

WORDS MATTER

Our words matter - more than we might realize until we examine and change them.

When we call something by a different name it changes the way we perceive and respond to it in our mind and body.

When my first marriage ended, my former partner began referring to me, not by my own lovely name, the one he'd said so affectionately when we were new and things were good and easy, but as "the bitch who left." I was *The Bitch Who Left*.

He was in pain, he was hurt and angry, and he was not yet clean or in recovery (which was the cause of our breakup, the perfect storm of our combined addictions and histories of unresolved trauma). He felt awful when we split up. He wanted to feel better so making me look and sound like a demon, a horrible person – that helped him feel better in contrast. *Good riddance*, he could say with confidence until he got into recovery and could admit it had been painful for him, and he, too, did the best he knew to do at the time. He stopped beating himself up and returned to calling me by my name.

So, let's start with that uncomfortable feeling we call a *Craving*.

Craving. Hmm, who taught us to call it that? Who benefits when we label any uncomfortable feeling a craving? Calling it a *craving* gives us just two choices, both of them stressful:

1. Use
2. Don't use.

When we do as we were trained and call discomfort a craving, we either ingest toxins and feel awful about that, or we experience withdrawal, agitation, and frustration and feel awful then, too!

Call the same feeling *Discomfort*, and suddenly you have a whole range of possibilities.

You could start brainstorming a list right now called *Things People Do to Feel More Comfortable*. It could become a very long list, especially when you put your head together with fellow buttkickers and others. Just start asking around. So many interesting conversations... So much freedom in all of those possibilities...

Ask everyone, *What do YOU do when you feel uncomfortable?* Suddenly there's a growing list of tools and tricks, instead of just one - the overused, proverbial hammer of the butt.

Speaking of 'the butt': why did we give it a fancy, sexy French name like *cigarette*?

Well, because we *didn't* give it that name, did we? The companies who manufacture it - and the rest of the PR bullshit that goes with it – gave it that name and, like obedient sheep, we followed along. *Just tell me what to do and what to call it.*

When we start calling them *Butts* instead, it sounds just a little less sexy to say I was putting yet another one in my mouth.

Here's another: the word *Smoking*.

There's a reason we say someone is *smokin' hot* – in part because of the way it sounds when we say it. *She is smokin' hot... whew*! We're drawn to words not only for their meaning but for their mouth feel - like food or anything else we hold in our mouth.

When we call it *sucking* (because that's what we're doing when we ingest tobacco in most forms) we see it for what it is. We are comforting ourselves in the way we did from the time we first showed up and latched on. Sucking is how we got our nourishment – it's how we survived and sustained life.

Sucking tobacco, though is another thing. It is not sustenance. It's toxin masked and chemically engineered to mimic sustenance in our neurophysiology and to make us feel like we need it to survive.

So let's call it *sucking*, shall we, and pair that with *butts*.

Some people will beat themselves up about their use of tobacco or nicotine. *I should never have started.* Or they'll refer to nicotine as something that has only done them harm and never good.

What I know for me, and expect for you, is that picking up butts in our youth was the best we knew to do at the time. My sense is it helped me survive an especially difficult time in my life at age 12, and at other times when I had few resources. It was the best I knew to do, just as leaving my marriage, in the presence of addiction and trauma, mine and his, was the best I knew to do at *that* time. Just as using other drugs was the best I knew to do at *that* time.

When we know better, we do better, said Maya Angelou. I'd add, *when we know better and have better and know we have better, we can do better*. So, staying connected and paying attention to the stories we tell ourselves and the words we use, will help us do better.

In that story we tell ourselves is another word that does us no good: *should* - as in, *I really should stop smoking*. Using the word *should* takes the power of our desire away from us and leaves us feeling lectured to, put upon and bossed around (*have to* and *must* have the same effect).

Within each of us is the desire - the fire - to kick and be free. So let's ignite that instead. Let's fan, protect and nurture that flame inside us.

Let's stop saying *should* to ourselves and each other and instead ask, *What do I really want? What's my true desire? Why do I want to be free?*

Wants. Focus there. No *shoulding* on ourselves or each other.

A word that puts some people off the process of kicking or even talking about it, is *addict* (and *addiction*). The truth is, all of these things we've reached for - whether the butts or other drugs or gambling -

anything we did obsessively or compulsively[1] was an attempt – our best attempt - to meet unmet needs. It was an attempt to comfort and soothe ourselves; to alleviate pain of some kind: emotional, physical, spiritual, whatever it may be.

So, when I talk with people about tobacco or nicotine, I ask them not about their addiction but about their *relationship* with tobacco or nicotine. It's turned out to be a completely different conversation that way. Most of us don't mind talking about a relationship, especially a difficult one!

While some are uncomfortable with the words *addict* or *addiction*, others are more than happy to call themselves an *addict*, and prefer that label or name over any other. It connects them to other addicts, and to a fellowship of recovery.

One more word: *quitting*. Who wants to be a quitter?

Stopping smoking was one of the hardest things I've ever done, especially because, at the time, I didn't know how hard it would be. As a result, like most people kicking, I gave myself nowhere near enough support for the process. No one was going to call **me** a *quitter*. The word that came as the years passed was one with more strength and presence, and that's *buttkicker*.

You're not a quitter. *Buttkicker* is a name we can feel proud to claim.

See how you do when you try substituting some words, notice how it feels in your body. Even changing small things, a little at a time, can make a big difference over time.

Name yourself free.

CHILDREN AND ANIMALS

Children and animals: they're some of our best teachers. Watch them.

Study them as your teachers.

They don't light things on fire and put them into their mouths - that is, unless some 'mature adult' taught them to do so. If they try something and don't like it (if it makes them cough and leaves a nasty taste in their mouth) they don't do it again – not until they reach an age when they're seeking comfort in new ways, or need to fit in so they force themselves to 'like' something because all their friends do.

Notice how creative and resourceful kids and animals are, especially when they feel stressed or want comfort. They cry – or bark - it out, they shake it off, and then, when they've done that, they let it go and move on. Amazing.

You were once this creative and wise, too. Could you ponder and ask, *How did I deal with stress when I was small? And, if tobacco and nicotine were simply not available to me, suddenly off the table or wiped from the face of the earth, what would I do today to face this day?*

By asking creative questions like this and observing these wise teachers around us, you can tap into your pre-tobacco, pre-nicotine, wise and creative self, too.

You, too, were once that free, and can be again in a whole new way.

Remember yourself free.

3

WHAT'S THAT IN YOUR MOUTH?

Be willing to put something else into your mouth. Suck on something besides a stick you've lit on fire, or a vape - a nicotine *crack pipe*, as Dr. Jill Williams calls it.

What else?

You tell me. We're human beings - creative by nature.

It's in your nature to be creative but it's also in your nature to seek easy comfort. So sometimes we head for the same-old, same-old.

If the same-old same-old was *truly* enough for you, though, you wouldn't be here, reading this now. I see you, the truth of you, beyond the habitual responding.

So, OK, I'll start the brainstorm and you can join

me. Here's my first list of ideas for what you might put in your mouth other than a lit stick:

- A pacifier.
- A bottle of water.
- A toothbrush (manual or electric).
- A toothpick: a stick that's not lit on fire.
- A stick of licorice (the actual root of the tree) or cinnamon
- A hunk of spicy ginger root
- Gum (nicotine or not; it's still better than an inhalant).
- A lozenge or a sweet (try xylitol; it's better for our teeth).
- A straw.
- Your own thumb.

Hey, now we're brainstorming!

OK, now it's your turn.

What are you putting into your mouth?

Mouth yourself free.

4

DRINK UP

Remember: You're mostly water so drink up.

Every time you take a whizz or sweat a drop, replace it.

For this purpose, carry water with you. **Bring bottles of water everywhere you go.** One for you, one for a thirsty friend.

Give sexy, refillable water bottles as gifts to other sexy buttkickers, too. Nothing says *I love you and I want you to stick around* like a sexy water bottle. Give one (or two?) to yourself. Get a bottle that comes with a straw and you'll also be working tool number 3 above – so double-bubble!

Drinking water makes everything work better. Every organ, every system in your body, thrives on hydration. It'll help you stay more grounded and resilient, instead of brittle and jittery.

Speaking of jittery, you may not want to hear this, but you may need to give up caffeine for a little while. Harsh, I know, but it's not the end of the world. You'll survive. Rooibos is one fine alternative; it's jam-packed with antioxidants and no caffeine. Look it up, bring it home and brew it up STRONG.

Get that water bottle. Fill it up. Suck it down. Hydrate. Stay gorgeous, inside and out.

Drink yourself free.

5

TO AIR IS HUMAN

To err is human. To breathe is divine.

Is there anything more divine, more luscious, more powerful than a deep, deep breath?

And it is totally free... until it isn't.

Breathe.

B r e a t h e.

Try this: put your fingers to your lips, without the butt in your mouth, and take a deep breath. Deeper. Now, blow it out as if you were blowing out smoke. Do that a few times, slowly. We call it *air dragging*. It satisfies some of the tactile experience, helps with focus, and the deep breathing soothes us, too.

Notice that you don't need the butt in your mouth to get a calming, invigorating effect.

Try this on your next fresh-air break. It works.

With practice, it works better and better.

Take another deep breath, this one slowly and though your nose. Notice how that feels. That's how we're meant to breathe most of the time, through our nose.

Do you know there are now entire books written and talks given about how to breathe? Because we forget that, too. Many of us never learned to do it properly.

Take another deep breath but this time, hold your nose and breathe in through a drinking straw. Feel that? That's what it feels like when we've waited too damn long to get free. We're fighting for breath; fighting for what was ours to begin with.

Breathe, deeply. In and out, right now, and smile.

Feel that? That's what it feels like to be free.

Breathe yourself free.

6

GET OUT OF THE WAY

Get out of your own way.

Stop telling yourself and everyone else what you can't do.

"But I can't stop…"

You create resistance by saying "I can't." You're driving with the brake on. Every time you say "I can't," you're hitting the brake. That takes more gas. That takes more effort. Suddenly you're on empty. And tired.

"I can't" is one of those stories that's of no use to you. When you say "I can't," the rest of your body believes it.

Besides, it's not true.

You can.

You're a miracle.

Your body is amazing; it heals itself, even without your help. **Without one conscious thought from you, your body has the wisdom to heal wounds.**

Your brain is as amazing.

It loves questions and fresh challenges and helping you sort things out, if you invite it and let it.

Your brain is constantly retooling and adapting to the information you feed it. It's seeking to make sense of things, even things that make no sense, like you sucking smoke into your lungs (and brain) over and over again.

"Well," it says, "I guess this is our normal now. I'd better adapt to it..."

Your brain, though, doesn't always know the difference between what is real and what isn't.

If you say, "I need, need, need to suck this junk into my lungs," your brain and the rest of you will adapt to that idea.

If you then say, "What the hell was I thinking? I love breathing! I love breathing fresh, clean, delicious air, and having more money! I'm a buttkicker now, and it feels GOOD," then your amazingly adaptive brain will (gratefully) adapt to that.

Fresh air? More of it? Yes, please!

Notice the ways you tell yourself things that hold your true self back.

Let them go, one by one.

Out with the old, in with the new.

Presto-change-o.

Change your mind… your words… yourself.

Look at you, over the course of your whole life thus far, and what you've lived through, dealt with and adapted to… some of it long before you ever lit a stick on fire and put it into your mouth as a way to cope with life.

You were free when you got here and you can be free again.

It starts with freeing your mind, one thought, one word at a time.

Change your mind free.

7

SEE IT, SAY IT, DRAW IT, SHARE IT, DO IT (AND LET IT DO YOU)

Many books on change will tell you to *find your why*.

And, yes of course you want to find your why – the biggest and most compelling reason you want to be free. What is *The Big Why* for you?

Now, let's take that a step further: write it out, then draw a picture of it and color it in. Give it legs to stand on and help it grow.

Start creating a vision of what YOU really want your life to look like. Now.

Not someone else's vision or truth; that's too simple. Yours.

Not the vision you chose years ago; the one that you want now.

If you don't know what it is now, just start asking the question. Your brain loves questions. Just start asking it these questions every day: *What do I want? What do I really, really want?*

Notice what you prefer. Let go of what you don't. The list can make itself.

Each time you get a clue about what you really want to do here, write that clue down. Find or make something to represent your vision. Carry that with you. If it's too big to carry with you, make or take a picture of it and carry that with you instead.

Draw your vision, too, your future, as well as your present tense, and chunk it down into smaller steps you can take to get from one to the other. Clear intent, then action.

Powerful.

Tell or show (or both) your vision to someone great who thinks you're great, too, to hold that vision with you. There's power in that, too. I'd LOVE to see and hear your butt-free vision[1].

See it, say it, draw it, share it, do it - a little at a time.

Notice your progress. Adjust. Fine tune. Repeat.

Then, each day, decide to feel as good as you can feel, even in the awkward experience of your newfound freedom. Imagine your perfect tomorrow the night before, and set that intention again at the start of the day. Imagine yourself enjoying the challenge of buttkicking, as you think ahead to your buttkicking. Have you ever enjoyed a challenge? Remember that. Write that down, too.

This is shaping up - shaping you up - to be your own personal buttkicking and *change-gonna-come* life vision. State it. Create it. Better yet: co-create it. Ask for and get the support you need - seen and unseen - to do so. It's your birthright.

Then you'll be able to put that butt down so you have both hands free to claim the support and your new life.

It's yours, waiting for you to arrive.

Vision yourself free (and loving it).

8

GO OUTSIDE AND PLAY

One day, that amazing body of yours will be like a pile of dirty laundry on the floor: lifeless, inert and smelly.

Right now, though, it isn't lifeless. It's pulsing with life.

Wanna get off your butts? Then it's time to get off your butt.

If you have enough life in you to read this (or to ignite things and put them into your mouth) you still have enough life in you to move your amazing body somehow and get your blood pumping and feed all of your organs.

Have you seen all the news stories that say, *Sitting is the new smoking*? Or the one that got popular in 2020, *Lonely is the new smoking*?

What then, if you're sitting, lonely *and* smoking? Holy smokes! Enough of that.

Let's get up, get outside and play.

Call it *exercise*, if you must.

Or call it *exorcise* (purging your demons) and clear all the accumulated stress of your day.

Call it whatever you like. Just get outside and do it. It doesn't need to be fancy or complicated or hard work. Go outside and do *anything.*

Do I need to say this again?

Apparently I do: You're still sitting still reading this, aren't you?

C'mon. Can you call a friend to go with you? Even phone to phone? Run around; Skip rope, like Rocky. Move like Jagger, Macklemore, Psy or Batiste; Do a bit of hula-hooping; Dance in the streets...

Here's one of my favorites, especially when I'm by myself: queue up some music that makes you feel like dancing, then take that mix out for a walk. Notice how your cadence changes, notice how you're smiling. Keep going. Then when you're tired out you can laugh at yourself and find a spot to lie down, maybe on the ground, and look up at the great big sky.

Feel like smoking? Nope. Me, neither. Not if you

played hard enough. That's how you'll know if you did.

Then take a nap. You'll probably need one. Some buttkickers sleep the entire first day that they're free.

Rest.

Repeat.

Play yourself free.

9

EAT A VEGETABLE. EAT A BEAN

Eat a vegetable. Eat a bean. Eat some fruit. Eat something that's still got some life in it (like you).

Things like greens and beans contain roughage. Roughage makes us tougher and more resilient. They clean your blood, help your gut and feed your head. They help make your muscles nice and strong, too.

You may still want to eat some dead things, too; we're not here to judge. We do need protein; what kind(s)? That's up to you and your body. Mix it up with things that are lively. Add some variety, vitamins and color. Try fewer white foods, the kind that can turn all pasty and slow in your gut and go with more of the other colors. Eat the rainbow.

Some foods are great because they don't taste

good with tobacco or nicotine. Notice what your taste buds are telling you as they wake up.

Some foods are great because they're cleansing, too. Leafy green veggies clean and strengthen the blood and everyplace the blood goes!

Some foods help us regulate our brain, feelings and emotions. There's a gut-brain connection: we're learning more about this every day.

And bump up the fiber… it's so cleansing. Go easy on the beans to start. The more you eat, the more you'll… produce fumes from the nether region! Though butt fumes would be an improvement on the butts' fumes, honestly! And another way to set boundaries.

If you're not already, take a good multivitamin. This will help you become and feel stronger, too. Add in psyllium to the mix, too.

You may notice some digestive sluggishness, especially when you first kick. I did. Fluids, veg, fruit, and other bulk-producing things like psyllium husk powder will help get the junk out of your system faster and more fully, leaving *you* feeling more like yourself a lot quicker.

If you can, get your vitamin D level checked. Getting enough Vitamin ;-D can have a profound and surprising effect on your energy level and mood, especially if your level's been low for a while (mine was).

Hey, you're in the process of changing your whole life here. Maybe you could try a new food each week, month or year?

Apple, Broccoli, Carrot and Pea,

Honeydew, Kiwi, Edamame, Green Tea,

I know you've got the picture,

You can close your eyes and see.

We won't spell out the whole alphabet here but you get the idea.

Buttkickers who fill up on foods like this may just be able to eat to their heart's content, stay leaner, get cleaner and feel more satisfied, as they – as you! - get free.

Eat yourself free.

LAUGH YOUR BUTT OFF

You don't always feel like laughing. You might feel like crying. Or screaming. Or giving up.

Sometimes we may *need* to scream, cry and rant but often a laugh is better than those three.

If you can make or let yourself laugh HARD for even thirty seconds, you can change your perspective, your brain chemistry - your actual, physical brain - without a single puff of smoke. Remember how I said the brain can't always tell real from imaginary? It works with laughing, too.

When you have the thought, *Oh, sucking on a lit stick would be nice right now*, laugh. Let it be a cue.

Laugh hard.

Then upload the thought, *What a ridiculous idea! What the hell was I thinking? I'm kicking those things!*

Laughing is a brain changer and a game changer. Keep a book in your pocket that makes you laugh when you read it – or have a 'funny' playlist lined up on YouTube or Spotify.

Most of us take ourselves very, very seriously which doesn't serve us well. Sometimes when I'm taking myself very seriously, if I'm lucky, I'll remember: *stop taking yourself so seriously, Nicci Tina. No one else does!*

Laugh yourself free.

11

LOOK CRAZY, GET SANE

Be willing to look a little *crazy* in the interest of getting sane.

As a person with some mental health challenges, I can sometimes get concerned with how I appear to others. But is anyone expecting me to have it all together? Are they? Really?

You can ask yourself that question, too. It's very liberating.

If the answer is *Yes*, you might then ask *Why*? Why would they expect that of you? And who is *they*?

People have watched you and me light toxins on fire for many years, ingesting them, as if that was normal. It isn't. It's weird. It's honestly weirder than most anything you or I could dream up as a way to get free.

So cry when you need to. Laugh when you can. Do some air drags. Put your arms around yourself and rock and hum. Put a pacifier in your mouth when you need to calm yourself down. Or your thumb.

Is it really cooler or more sane to light something on fire and suck the smoke out of it into your amazing, human body?

Really? What industry taught us that was cool or normal, and what do they care about your amazing, human body?

I love your body. I'd love for you to love it, too. So much so that you'll question anyone or anything that would advocate (or advertise) for you to do anything that doesn't give it the straight up 100% adoration it deserves. So much so that you'll love on it, even in public, even if that looks weirder than weird. Put your arms around yourself right now – yes, even if you are reading this on a bus and people are looking. Most of us need a lot more hugs that we give ourselves and each other, especially nowadays.

Stop letting other people - including a bunch of fancypants advertising execs - dictate what's smart and sane and hip and cool and sexy and You.

When they try – as they will – you can laugh at them, too.

What's crazy? You tell me.

Define yourself free.

12

TAP YOURSELF FREE

Tap into your own natural resources and some ancient wisdom.

Tapping on the same meridian points on the body that have been used in acupuncture and more for, like, ever, can help heal all kinds of physical and emotional ailments. Acupuncture is great, but you do need an appointment or an abundance of training to do it properly. Tapping is a less exact practice, to be sure, but you can do it yourself, on yourself, and without the needles. Tapping is one of the practices where persistence can pay high dividends.

Here's another exciting thing about tapping: **you can tap yourself ready if you're not ready to tap yourself free.**

I almost feel like shouting this from the rooftops or going ALL CAPS and **BOLD** here because this means **you can kick gradually**.

TAPPING CAN HELP YOU GET READY TO GET READY TO GET FREE.

One of the most stressful things about kicking for most of us is the idea that we need to do it all at once. Many of us were told, "You need to set and commit to a quit date." We tried that; it was so unnecessarily stressful and traumatizing. Some of us tried cutting down. It worked for some, but many of us had no luck whatsoever with cutting down to zero over the long haul. So we came to believe that we needed to kick completely and suddenly to get free. That is simply not true anymore.

This fact is the single most important and exciting thing I've discovered in the thirty years I've been practicing and teaching buttkicking. **You can kick gradually.** You can be in the process of kicking while you continue to use.

Let that sink in.

This is how to tap in a way that will rock your buttkicking world.

Tap when you're the most uncomfortable, i.e. when you have the urge to dip, chew or fire one up.

Tap when you're in situations when things are coming up that feel uncomfortable, frustrating, triggering.

Tap between the urge and the act of using, in whatever form.

Those words are pure gold.

You can watch our video – wow, now ten years old! - **Tap Yourself Free**[1] to see how. Watch the video, and tap through that sequence - each and every time - before you light up. Download the chart on our Patreon or Facebook page. Tap along with us. Do it.

Tap and release, little by little by little.

Of course it looks weird and feels strange to begin with - until it doesn't.

So did sucking butts. You don't remember this – unless you do – but when you were small and innocent and wise and saw someone with smoke or vapor rolling out of their mouth for the first time, that looked weird. It was like nothing you had ever seen before.

Before you knew it, it looked normal. That's what we call programming. It happens every day. We're trained, indoctrinated to see some things as sane and normal, and others as weird and crazy.

If every time you saw someone tapping in response to discomfort instead of seeing smoke flowing out of their mouth, or big clouds of vapor, or thick brown spit, then tapping would be as normal to you as a smile or a hug or an encouraging word ought to be. It's all about how we're trained. Fortunately, seeing this, we can retrain ourselves... and we can do that gradually, too.

It's thrilling.

When I first tapped, I tested it behind closed doors in my own home. I told no one what I was doing. When I realized it worked, I started sharing it with clients, in the privacy of their session, and again, behind closed doors. By the time I wrote the first edition of this book in 2011, I had started tapping in presentations with fellow healthcare providers and in coffee houses with friends, tapping along.

Adapting from a perspective that said smoking is normal to one that said smoking is weird, and to see tapping as normal took me many years. It doesn't need to take you as long. Adapting is how we evolve, and tapping can help us do that, too.

Try it on everything. That's what the founder once suggested. It's free. As we are all too well aware, tobacco is not free; it's expensive and it's costly, too. Hey, maybe you could tap yourself rich, too!

You have so much power in your own hands... if you knew how much, it might startle you.

Find out. You can handle the truth.

Tap yourself free.

13

COME OUT, COME OUT,
WHEREVER YOU ARE

In the ten years since the first edition of this book, the biggest surprise has been the number of people I've met who are closeted. Closeted smokers, chewers and vapers, that is.

Although some people still use tobacco and nicotine with abandon, billowing and spitting openly, out in the streets, some – many more than you'd imagine - are using with secrecy and shame. So much so, they'll even refer to themselves as closeted.

These are estheticians, energy workers, massage and mental health therapists. They are surgeons, nurses, dentists, hygienists... they're represented in every healthcare profession. They are parents. They are clergy and they are coaches. They are athletes, young and older. Some are out to one friend, family member or co-worker; some are out to no one. Some are out on the weekends, in the company of a few adults, saying things like, *I really only smoke when I drink. It's a social thing.* Others are back-alley, in-the-cellar, behind-the-barn users only, with no witnesses, ever.

They go to great lengths to mask their use. This includes hosing themselves down with air fresheners, (on top of the secondhand smoke), brushing and using mouthwash after each one, and even changing clothes several times a day. Some have smoking clothes they change into and out of each time they use, all day long.

Some say it feels like having another personality, there's such a split between the way they appear to live their lives and the way they, in fact, do.

I share this with you not to out anyone; it's hard enough already to be closeted. It's also hard enough to be using and going through all these gyrations to keep it going. Using, and keeping your using a secret too, that's exhausting, I'm told, and can well imagine.

I want you to know that, if you're closeted, you can reach out to me via DM or Messenger on social media: Facebook[1], Instagram[2], and LinkedIn[3]. You can attend 12 Step fellowship Zoom calls, too, anonymously. You can change your name as you log in and leave your camera off. No one needs to know it's you. There's help for you, and you never need to say your name or show your face.

And I hope one day you'll find the liberation some of us have found in coming out of our closets and telling the truth about who we are, where we've been, and how we live.

When you out yourself, and say, *I've been struggling with this*, you free yourself, and you free others to do the same.

There are so many of us out here to support you through this.

Out yourself free...

But if you're not ready for that, just know you can out yourself to me. Many have; I've never told their names. They each got great relief knowing they weren't alone in this. Many then went on to kick, come out and stay free. Closets don't make secrets go away; they just make them go deeper. You have a choice.

Come on out. The air is much better out here.

Out yourself free.

14

NO MORE NICE DEAD PEOPLE

It's time: you can stop silencing your anger, fear and frustration with a smoky pacifier.

Some of us know we've been doing this over the years; silencing our true feelings and *shushing* ourselves, making nice-nice and shutting things down, when we feel like blowing things up.

Some of us discover the powder keg we've been plugging up for decades, after we kick. The people around us might be so put-off, stunned or afraid of our anger that they'll suggest we go back to smoking. They may even go another step and buy us a pack. That's happened. Or, we may feel the same and go out and buy some for ourselves. That happens a lot.

As wonderful a world as it is that we live in, there's also plenty in the world to be angry about.

Our anger is meant to be expressed, used and transformed somehow, and in a way that doesn't burn others, or us.

How?

We need to get real and we need to get skills so that our anger doesn't come out sideways, armed and flailing, all at the same time. Smoking feeds on regret, amongst other things. And regret feeds on smoking, too, so we want to break that cycle.

How?

Learning how to effectively express our anger and the other feelings that are alive and kicking in us could save us our freedom, and can save us not only from nicotine, but from incarceration, too. Who wants to put down smoking to pick up charges?

And, anger, like other feelings, is part of what makes us real and alive and uniquely ourselves. It's part of our range of normal human feeling states.

Dr. Marshall Rosenberg once said, "We are not in this world to be nice, dead people." But Marshall also knew that most of us didn't learn the skills or language to do otherwise. From a very early age, most of us learned instead to suck it up; to live within a limited range of feelings and emotional expression; to be seen and not heard; to say something nice or say nothing at all…. and more ridiculous, violent bullshit like that. **Anything that robs us of what's alive in us, the life in us,** Marshall would say, **is violent.**

Seeing this, Marshall created a way for *every* feeling that's alive in us to be expressed, safely, and in a way that's win-win.

He called this practice Nonviolent Communication[1], or NVC.

Like 12 Steps groups, and the buttkicking community, NVC is available online or in face-to-face groups. There you can practice and play with this way of telling the truth and not getting in trouble for it; asking for what you want and winning; setting boundaries without the need for a giant cloud of smoke.

The giraffe is a symbol of Nonviolent Communication: A long neck for perspective, the largest heart of any land mammal, and saliva so powerful it can dissolve thorns. What most people won't tell you is that the giraffe also has a kick so strong, it can kill a lion. NVC is like that, too. It's so powerful that it can knock the butt right out of your mouth (as you learn how to meet your needs without nicotine) and you'll say Thank You.

Think of NVC as Verbal Aikido. This really is a language: a practice of being real, and not so nicey-nice all the time.

Then we can take the silencer out of our mouth, for good.

Find NVC.

NVC yourself free.

15

DO THE MATH

Do the math, they said.

When I was still smoking, in one of the many stop smoking classes and workshops I took back then, they had us get out our calculators and actually do the math.

Too bad I hadn't learned NVC back then (see Chapter 14) because I was pretty mad that anyone would even suggest such a thing. Do the math?! Wasn't this painful enough already, *without* doing the math?

Nope, it wasn't, clearly, because I was still smoking then, and pretty mindlessly. I could tell you the cost of a pack, and the three closest places to buy one cheaply, but I'd never tallied that up over a month or longer. Doing the math took it from mindless to more mindful. It was part of getting real; yet another step in the process of getting free.

Doing the math was another step in the process of being willing to go to any lengths to get and stay free.

Do you know how much you spend in a year on tobacco or nicotine? We're just talking cash money here – leave the health costs out of it for the moment. Just stop and calculate it, now.

After you do, write that down and look at it. For many of us, this is the first time we've ever looked at that number.

Now, multiply that number times three. Then, multiply that number times five. Write those numbers, too.

The next three to five years will go by, whether you kick or not; whether we're healthy or not to enjoy them; whether we're here or not to experience them.

In one of those classes, a woman next to me did her calculation, and when she saw the number she stared at it and her eyes filled up with tears. Then she got so angry to be crying that she got up and walked out of the class. She came back to the class after about 15 minutes, during which time she smoked about five cigarettes, judging by the time it took and the way she was breathing. She sat back down in her chair and then she said, "I'm done. That's it."

She told the class that she was paying **twice** her car payment each month in what she paid for cigarettes, and she didn't have a car anymore because it had been repossessed. She realized when she *did the math* that she'd been buying cigarettes instead of making her car payment, but not until that moment.

Denial is a powerful thing, dear friend. A multinational industry is built on our denial and our dollars. I smoked for decades. It adds up. It can add up to one more reason for us to kick and stay free, too.

Do the math.

Calculate yourself free.

16

BETTER LIVING THROUGH BETTER CHEMISTRY (OR TO NICOTINE OR NOT TO NICOTINE)

This is a controversial one.

Ten years ago, vaping was barely a thing. Now it's an industry in the multi-billions in the US alone, and most are owned and sold by the tobacco industry which is still a popular stock investment. People are making some serious bank on the not-yet-butt-kickers amongst us who continue to fund it and defund themselves.

We're not focused there – we're focused on you getting free, as free as you want to be and as fast as you want to be there.

Ten years ago, I was two thumbs-up on nicotine replacement therapies (NRTs). I didn't comment on vaping then because there were still too many uncertainties and concerns with it[1] but the gum, patches, and lozenges – I did say Yes to those, following the guidance of experts in the field like Dr. Jill Williams who'd said, It's the smoke that kills[2]."

Now, ten years later, I'm on the fence about NRTs.

I know many who have kicked smoking and nicotine using NRTs as a bridge to stop smoking and eventually nicotine, too. I know some who go back and forth between NRTs and tobacco, depending on availability and their level of discomfort. On a good day, they can stick to the NRTs. On a tougher day, they're back to the smoke or vape pen, and feeling stuck again. I've met some who are chewing the gum, wearing the patch, and tearing off the patch to smoke or vape and then slapping it back on again afterwards. Their nicotine levels are through the roof.

A growing number of people come to me for help with kicking vaping. Still more now tell me they're addicted to *both* smoking and vaping and more addicted than ever.

Some doctors see vaping as poison; others are, in fact, prescribing it, seeing it as harm reduction.

I see some people vaping (and coughing) in a way that scared me away from vaping in the way watching people use crack cocaine scared me away from that. Sometimes our fear is a useful thing.

All of this to say: I'm now a stronger advocate for other kinds of chemistry, including antidepressant medication. This, too, is subject to change. If there was research tomorrow damning it, I'd definitely want to learn more. At this writing, we've just found out that one smoking cessation drug may be carcinogenic. More research is necessary to know for certain. I'm grateful I'd never recommended that one.

When I was in rehab back in the day, I was offered antidepressant medication. I declined, saying I'd come there to get free, not a new drug. I was there to feel and heal as much as possible in those 30 days. Since the first edition of *Buttkickers*, I took antidepressant medication for several years; I found benefit in it. I was grateful it was there. It was a difficult time, and I couldn't seem to do the things I knew I needed to do to feel better.

Then, when I increased my movement – which the medication probably helped me to do - and got back to daily prayer and meditation, and got myself back to 12 Step fellowships, connecting daily, and started hosting Zoom calls, too, and being of service in those places, the need for the medication went away. I stopped taking it a while ago. It had given me the bridge I needed to do the other things I needed to do. It helped to jostle me out of a deep slump. No regrets: I'd pick up anti-depressant medication again if I found myself there, overwhelmed and struggling, again. It was a bridge to a better life – not a substitute for co-creating that life.

Some tell me a vape pen was a bridge to freedom for them, and some swear by NRTs – gum, lozenges or the patch - as the thing that helped get them totally smoke *and* nicotine free. Some tell me they feel free on nicotine; others say they didn't feel truly free until they were nicotine-free, too.

So, there's my story and some experiences of others. Keep asking others. Ask about meds, too, if that makes sense for you. Ask, listen and learn, and watch people, too. See what you see. Do your own research. In my mind, this – buttkicking - is all about freedom, and what *you* call freedom, for you.

One thing we know for sure is that a cigarette combusts neurotoxins fueled by additives like ammonia that rapidly cross the blood-brain barrier. We know that testing for the presence of it in your system is a CO - carbon monoxide – screen. Yes, that's the same toxicology test used to determine one's level of carbon monoxide poisoning – you know, if a heater malfunctions or you run your car in an enclosed space and fill the place with exhaust fumes. Carbon monoxide is a lethal substance. Inhaling it is clearly not living better through chemistry.

We can **definitely** do better than that. You'll choose what's right for you, and if it doesn't work out the way you like, you can try something else.

Research yourself free.

QUESTION AUTHORITY

Question authority, including your own.

Especially your own.

Are you telling yourself something – anything - that isn't serving you? Is there a chance - even the slightest chance (even a chance in hell) - that it isn't true? If so, why keep repeating the thought? Why keep feeding a thought that's not feeding you back?

We do this with many things and many of us – millions - when it comes to nicotine and tobacco.

For years and years, from the first time I tried to kick at 16, I said over and over, *I can't stop smoking.* I said it so many times, to other people and to myself, I had a robust neural pathway that was lined with signs that said, *I can't stop smoking.* It was a neural pathway paved in tar, a veritable superhighway with giant flashing signs that said *I Can't Stop Smoking.*

Who was served by that story? Or the story of, *I need a cigarette?*

How many millions of times did I say that rubbish?

I needed comfort, I needed support, I needed help with healing trauma, with treating my depression, help with my focus and executive function. I sure as hell didn't need a blend of combustible neurotoxins. At 12 – it was the best I knew to do. Decades later, I was just settling, and telling stories, stories that helped no one, least of all me.

Add to that neural superhighway the number of times I'd also said, *I enjoy smoking. I don't really want to stop.* That's one thing that I and others say when we decide to just give up and give in and tell ourselves we're enjoying getting beat up and paying for it.

Is it possible that some people really do enjoy smoking, chewing, spitting and vaping and don't want to stop? Yes, of course. I know there are. It's pretty compelling, as we know. It's engineered to be compelling, and the industry's relentless marketing and product placement - in movies and with online influencers – steadily shapes our thinking, too.

For a while, I believed I was one of those *I'm enjoying this* people. On another level, though, I wanted out and didn't know how. It felt better to say that was what I wanted - to convince myself of that - rather than feeling out of control. There was a part of me that bought that story: hook, line and sinker.

There was another part that was not buying any of that, and was relieved when I finally said, "Actually, I'm powerless to kick this under my own steam. That's the fact of the matter. It's stealing my life, one drag, one hit at a time." This was a story that did serve me, because then I became teachable, and I could find the right help to get out.

So although there was a story about enjoyment for a while, at the heart of the matter it was straight-up fiction. On a deeper level I felt like I was stuck, day after day, in an abusive relationship with a partner who was poisoning me *but just a little bit* every day. I was paying for that with my own hard-earned money while telling myself and everyone who'd listen that we were into each other. It was like financially supporting a partner who abuses you because you like the idea of being in a relationship, or because the sex is good sometimes.

The first time I met someone who confessed to me that she'd done that with an actual human partner, I had a moment of thinking, *Oh my God, how sad! Never.*

There was a story. Sometime later I thought, *Wow, damn. I've been doing that, too... and for a helluva lot longer than she has.*

These are just two examples of stories I told myself, over and over, like meditation mantras, that weren't serving me. *I can't kick; it's too hard*, and *I'm enjoying this; it's worth it.*

The truth for me and for many is: we *weren't* enjoying it quite as much as we said we did. We *could* kick, it *wasn't* too hard if we did it with support while we supported others, and we *were* worth the trouble. Kicking - however hard it might be - is a worthy challenge (you like a worthy challenge, don't you?) and we can start betting on ourselves, and back it up with our words, our actions and our connections.

I could tell you a hundred stories now of people you'd think could never kick – they told me they couldn't - who have now kicked and transformed their lives. The true story is, if you truly want to kick, you can, too. And that's a fact.

The number one game changer – the new and true story - for me became: I don't do things like kicking alone. *I take names* (see Chapter 20) and plenty of 'em. Lots of names.

We get ourselves a pack of people, instead of a pack of poison and a pack of lies.

I'm now part of *your* pack of people. NicciTina is on your list of names. And, if I tell you a story that's not serving you, by all means, question my authority, too!

I'm a fellow traveler, another buttkicker on the bus. There's loads I don't know about life and how things work. And I'm one buttkicker who knows a thing or two - now - about buttkicking, having done it myself and with others for decades. There was a point when I couldn't stop and was stuck in it, thinking and telling others I'd never get out. I would have bet against myself; that's how convinced I was. I think that those of us who do get out need to help others do the same, even if it's just by saying, *I believe in you; you can do this,* and *here's what's worked for me.*

And not everything I tell you worked for everyone else I've known. Some things work for some of us, other things work for others of us. This is another reason why it is so important to question authority, especially anyone who pitches us a one-size-fits-all mindset. We can each look around us and see that's not the case! We are each living proof, aren't we, that not everything works for everybody. We're individuals, not cookie-cutter cookies, cookie.

Asking questions helps us get fresh perspective. Question every single thing that's got some stress in it. *Is this really as stressful as I'm making it? How could I make it less so?*

Question every single thing you spend your money on. *How is this serving me? What impact is it having?*

Question every single thing that's messing with your health, wealth and especially the health-wealth.

Questioning is one of the ways we take our freedom back.

Question yourself free.

18

BREAK – OR MAKE – THE TRANCE

If you have a story about your relationship with tobacco or nicotine that's not serving you, you could be maintaining **a self-induced trance**.

Strong words, eh?

Not as strong as you think. Have you ever driven your car or ridden on transit and couldn't remember getting from Point A to Point B? Yes? Then you're already quite familiar with your own DIY trance induction.

Those of us who have experienced trauma have often used trance – unconsciously, and wisely, I would say - as a way to escape the intensity of a situation, especially when we couldn't physically remove ourselves from it. Trance, in that way, has been one of the many ways we've survived.

Chances are, you've experienced and survived trauma. I'll go a step further and say: I believe everyone who is still using tobacco or nicotine today has experienced trauma.

I'll go another step further than that and say: I believe everyone alive on this planet has experienced some trauma. Some of us use tobacco and nicotine as a way to cope, manage or check out from the effects of that trauma.

And we also use trance states. And often we use them together.

A trance state can serve our survival *and also our intentions*, such as when people have hypnotherapy to kick butts. We can also use trance states to kick butts and transform our lives when we have a daily meditation practice and when we tap - that, too, can have a healthy, trance-like quality to it. And it's free, and in our own hands.

So, just as we've slipped into trance states to survive or to continue using tobacco or nicotine, we can use trance states to kick, stay free and grow.

We can break trance states, too.

When we resolve to only use tobacco or nicotine consciously, and do absolutely nothing else at the same time, this will help us break the unconscious using trance. Multitasking along with our use disconnects us from what we're doing. It also pairs – connects - our using with everything else we do at the same time.

So, we want to unpair things, whatever you've had it paired with: waking, coffee, tea, booze, driving, texting, talking face-to-face or on the phone, post-meal, post-sex; pre-, during and post-everything. We stop using it as a reward, as punctuation, or as an accompaniment.

So, when you do use, do nothing else at the same time and use as consciously as possible.

For some, this single change – unpairing, and only using consciously - has done the trick to deliver the kick.

As one conscious buttkicker celebrating a year of freedom said, "Once I stopped using it with every other thing I did, I noticed how foul, how filthy it tasted. I noticed how much time I'd spent doing it. That was it. I was done, over it." She was free then to live the rest of her life more consciously and intentionally. You can, too.

Wake yourself free.

19

THE GRAND ADVENTURE

During three decades of buttkicking - my own and that of others - I've met thousands of people in varying stages of getting free. I've heard as many stories in response to the question, *How did YOU do it?*

One great story came from a man who was a regular at one of the groups I'd visited. He'd been off-and-on kicking for a while when we met.

He said, "I dreaded it for a long time. That attitude never got me what I wanted. One night, I thought back on my life and all of the times I'd done things I didn't really want to do, and how I felt proud afterwards."

"I thought about when I was flying. I was a fighter pilot." He touched his jacket. He still wore the flight jacket that was his when he was flying. It was beautiful, well-worn yet well-preserved. "I felt so ready, doing all of my training, but when it was time to go on my first mission, I felt the fear rising in me... I knew I had to combat that or it would have me. The thought came to me to see the mission as an adventure. That – and the rest of my training, and friends, too - got me through."

"At some point, I started to see my whole life that way, as a grand adventure, but it had never occurred to me to approach stopping smoking that way - in part because I saw it as stopping something, instead of doing something, like a quitter.

"As you say, *I'm not a quitter*, well, I'm not a quitter, either. Seeing kicking as something I was doing, instead of something I was stopping doing - that helped me to see kicking as part of The Grand Adventure."

Another story influenced my own kick. This was an old man of the sea in Maine where I'm from and where I'd returned to at the time I was kicking. He would say to me, in his Mainer accent, "As far as I'm concerned, if you don't know when you had your last cigarette, then maybe you haven't had your last cigarette."

That thought, combined with the idea someone

else had offered, to stop setting quit dates and just see how long I could go each time I set them down, combined to kick off my kicking.

Each time I set out again, to see how long I could go and learn what I could learn along the way, I'd write the time - and later the date, too - on a piece of paper. In the early days, I didn't need to write the date because I wasn't making it beyond that day. I'd just cobble together a few rough hours before I'd light up again. But still, each time I did this, I'd just see how long I could go, and what I could learn each time. I don't call it a *try*. *Adventure* is a good word. It's good, too, because buttkicking is an adventure.

Buttkicking *required* me to transform my life, in the best ways possible, and it *resulted* in changing my life, also in the best ways possible.

So, no more quit dates. Just see how long you can go each time, and treat each time as an adventure, and notice what you're learning. And make sure you bring plenty of snacks, plenty of ways to treat, reward, comfort and nurture yourself, along the way. No more cold turkey approaches to kicking, please! It just leaves us feeing deprived and super cranky.

I was so stingy and pushy with myself when I

kicked. Awful, like a buttkicking drill sergeant with a brand new recruit, or a mean Mommy to my inner child. If I had it to do again, I'd splurge and indulge as much as I could: snuggly snoozes and bubble baths, mani-pedis and long walks and talks with friends... it doesn't have to be expensive to treat ourselves right on this – our – hero's journey.

Let's be generous with ourselves on this adventure. Let's feel GOOD when we're on it. If we can't go to some expensive spa to kick, we can do our best to create our own!

And, this isn't just a buttkicking adventure; if we do it right, it's also some damn good science.

Each time we set the butts down and walk away, it's an adventure, and there's always learning in it, too. In the movie, The Martian, the lead character, stuck alone in his adventure on Mars said, "In the face of overwhelming odds, I'm left with only one option: I'm going to have to science the shit out of this."

You, too, can *science the shit* out of *your* other-worldly buttkicking adventure.

See how long you can go, make sure you write down the day and time each time you set them down, and just see what each adventure can teach you. See what you can learn about yourself and the world around you when you take the butts off the table as an option. You'll find out how creative, bold and loving you truly are and can be.

Adventure yourself free.

KICK BUTTS, TAKE NAMES

Once you're on the path of kicking, the best way I've found to make kicking stick is to help somebody else kick, even while you're early in the process of kicking. You want someone ahead of you on the path, and someone coming up alongside you. As you read those words, can you imagine how different that could feel, how different it is from doing it all alone?

This is the number one tip, if you ask me. The other 19 are good, but this is the gem, the *piece de resistance*. So of course I put in the back, because if you're anything like me, you either go to the back of a book like this and read that first, or you enjoy the slow build to the finale.

This one tip is like twenty rolled into one.

They say if you really want to learn something

well, teach it to somebody else. And, I'd add, let others teach you by example.

When I was celebrating just a month without tobacco, someone asked me to come up alongside her kicking, too. *But,* I said, *that woman over there, she's got a whole year free.* This newcomer said she felt like I could relate to her, and she could better relate to me. It was still fresh for me, she said, and that woman with a whole year, that just seemed so far away.

So I helped her, and honestly, she helped me as much. Everything she asked me, if I didn't have an answer, I'd see what I could learn about it. I'd look it up. I'd ask the woman with a whole year. I'd ask the fisherman dude.

As time passed and we all stayed in each other's lives, each one of us was weaving our part in this web of interconnection. We wanted to be strong and keep kicking for each other, sometimes even more than we wanted to stay the course for ourselves. When I'd think about giving up, giving in, in those moments when I felt alone and as if none of it mattered, I'd think about who else might give up if I did.

This wasn't just about me anymore. It was about us, all of us. People I'd met and people I'd yet to meet. The web grew ever stronger and supported us all. It's still growing.

I do all I can to keep the memory of what it felt like then as fresh as possible now. I tell the story of what it was like, what happened, and what it's like today, regularly.

So take names of people who can help and guide you, and become a name for others, too. Names of people, and names of things you can reach out to for comfort and support, too. Take those names down and keep them close. Get someone ahead of you and someone you're helping come up alongside. Buffer yourself with support, so the world and kicking doesn't feel so overwhelming. That's how we change our world, that's how the world changes. Get a ton of support and wrap it around you.

Have you ever noticed how a single hug at the right moment can give you a sigh of relief, of release? Or when you say, "Would you just listen…" and that request is met with true listening? It's huge, right? Transformative.

You're doing this yourself but you're not doing it alone anymore.

As fellow travelers on this road to freedom and in the process of transformation, we give each other not only the gift of companioning as we go; we also give each other the massive gift of perspective.

When you're standing in the middle of anything – especially in a challenging time – it's simply not possible to have true perspective. But another person who sees you, who truly sees the light in you *and* your bullshit, too, can give you the gift of seeing the best and most ridiculous ideas and aspects of yourself, maybe in a way that makes you smile and even laugh at the same time. And the best way to cultivate and participate in relationships like this is to keep coming back to them, to each other. Then we can keep coming back to ourselves, to our senses, to our best life.

And, when we keep coming back to our village, our team, our pack or our tribe, we can better see our own light and bullshit in the light and shadow, brilliance and bullshit of each other's, too. Sometimes you'll see someone else say or do something so wise or weird and think, *Oh, I'm like that. too!* Or, *Whoa! I'm so damn glad I don't do <u>that</u> anymore!*

So this 20th tool is: find your pack. If Google, Instagram, Facebook or asking around doesn't get you there and you need help to find your pack, let me know. Once you find your pack, get yourself in the middle of it. Don't do this alone. We weren't meant to go it or grow alone. We get these big challenges to connect us with one another in meaningful ways. Your challenge and learning is meant to serve another, as is mine. That's why I'm still in mutual support communities, on a path to keep evolving and loving, and it's why I wrote this book. For your evolving, loving and service, too.

Love yourself - and others - free. Together we can do what no one of us can do alone.

IN SUMMARY

At the start of this book, I asked you a question, one that came to me as I sat down to write this the first time on 11 -11 -11.

Are you willing to forget every single useless thing you've learned in the interest of remembering the truth of who you are?

Here's one bit of truth I want to offer: this isn't really about tobacco or nicotine at all. We use and we use, but honestly, if we were getting what we needed there, it wouldn't be a problem.

Someone once told me, "Y'know, you can never get enough of what you don't really want."

When we pair that thought with another observation about our relationship with tobacco, nicotine and more, **One is too many and a thousand is never enough**, we see it's because it isn't filling us up the way we truly yearn to be filled up and fulfilled.

Tobacco, nicotine can't fulfil us. It's not what we're truly yearning for. It's not what our body, mind and spirit really want or need to be nourished and satisfied. **It's a cheap (and costly) substitute for what we really want and need.** What we want and need is less expensive – it's free - and even more available to us than tobacco or nicotine.

Tobacco, nicotine is not the real solution to anything. It's also not the real problem.

The one billion plus people on this planet using it - that's a manifestation of a problem. It's an outgrowth of a problem.

The true problem is our disconnection: from each other, from our true selves, from our purpose, from our direction, from hope, from the sense of something greater that unites us all – from life itself - and from our own light. Our shiny bumbling brilliance.

My friend Jim Roi is fond of saying, *We're like drunken gods.*

We're meant to be these amazing, co-creative

fireballs of energy, made of the same stuff as the stars, yet we've traded our fire and light for the light at the end of a stick.

So, wrapping this up: this is not the end of the process, nor is it the beginning.

You started the process of buttkicking before you'd even picked up this book. Picking up this book was just one step in the process, preceded by the desire that helped to put this book in your hands, and the curiosity that led to you opening it, and opening yourself to it.

And it's definitely not the conclusion, either. Even if you kicked while you were reading this book, as some have, this is still just a step – or a series of steps, of actions you've taken - in the process of transforming your life, of taking owner-ship, on another, deeper level, of your life.

This is not when I say, *time to smoke your last cigarette!* Or *time to set your 'quit date'!* Or time to do anything you haven't decided to do. This is a very individual process. We're learning to respect and truly honor our own individuality, in our butt-kicking and in all areas of our lives.

My sense is, if you'll do these things, from this moment forward:

- tune in and tap (healthy wealthy trance induction) in between *each and every* urge and act of using
- use consciously, single-handedly, doing nothing else - no multitasking - while using tobacco or nicotine - not even social media, a book, a song, a chat or a beverage
- respond to each urge with love and action, not with deprivation
- treat the process of buttkicking as *a bold and loving adventure*
- stop setting quit dates and just see how long you can go each time you set it down. Keep track and stay curious, see what you've learned each time you pick it up again (if you do)
- respect your own individual process – embrace your pace – and your own individuality and let your own personal buttkicking freedom find you and meet you on the path

If you'll do just these few, simple, moment to moment, breath to breath changes … they may just - you can let them - turn the lock and deliver you the freedom, health, wealth and buttkicking satisfaction you've been seeking, in your own time.

And even *as* you do these things, you can begin to **help others do the same**, even just one person to start, which will **give your intent and freedom a firmer foundation** for the rest of your buttkicking, ever-evolving, ever-loving life. **When we teach what we're learning, we learn it more deeply and fully**. When we're of service to others in meaningful ways, it serves our own life as well. As long as we do so in balance with the rest of our lives.

And some of us buttkickers will want the rest of the tips and tools herein; a big, full toolbox. And some will need to read a few (or a lot) more books about kicking or attend some workshops and seminars. Many of us will seek and find additional help and helpers for the growing, healing and transforming of our lives, through healthcare professionals and through other teachers and guides.

Some will go it alone, preferring that (which truly baffles me, but to each their own).

Others of us will find a tribe to grow and transform together, in places like 12 Step fellowships and other dynamic, fun and mutually nurturing communities.

So I do hope you'll honor your own individuality in this process and in the transformation of your life. And in my heart of hearts, I'm hoping I'll get the chance to meet you one day, in one of the rooms or in the streets.

Although the freedom, healing and improved health-wealth of buttkicking are all thrilling, the best part of buttkicking for me – besides the complete transformation it brings with it - has been the chance to stick around and share it. I'm glad and grateful I could share some of what I've learned over these last thirty years with you.

For each of these ways of leaving tobacco, there's been at least one person who's told me *this one* or another or three was their tipping point to freedom.

For many of these tools, there's been someone who told me they didn't think it was of enough value to have in a book. To each their own. If you found yours here, I could not be more delighted. If you didn't, I'm hoping one of these will help you brainstorm your own or lead you to the help you need to go the next step in your own journey to buttkicking freedom.

And, if none of these gets it done, there are more books out there *and* more being written, including the 3rd edition of *Kick Butts Take Names*!

One way or another, you can get free. I'm 100% sure of it. Lean into my faith in you until you find your own.

You can do this, and do it your way. Millions have before you and me. You can, too.

ACKNOWLEDGMENTS

Thanks to… where do I begin?

So many times I've moaned and wept about the pain of doing this Kick Butts Take Names thing all alone.

Writing and activism - like buttkicking - can feel pretty damn lonesome.

Then I sat down to write acknowledgements – who helped this happen? - and the names just kept showing up on the page.

Some of you have contributed to the Patreon, others have shown up in other ways that fed, inspired, and cheered on this work. Some of you will wonder why you're on this list, others will say - and rightfully so - *Oh, I'd better be on that Acknowledgments page!*

You all belong here. As do others whose names I'd never learned, or have (probably) forgotten to mention.

Thank you to my partner, "my sweet Lor" Campbell; to my mom, stepmom, mum-in-law, godmother and grandmothers, all of you powerhouses, each in your own way; to the two great men I call Dad: to my fellow writers and buttkickers, in and outside the rooms, some of you are listed here; to my 12 Step fellowships and fellow travelers, and to my HP, without which there'd be no book at all, and no me to write it.

And thanks to: CiCi YusiRianti Adji, Edward Aguayo, Cossette Ahlborn, Gonca Akgul, Onur Aksoy, Yuliya Aldridge, Lesia Alexander, Mohammed Amir, Cathie Anderson, Kaitlin Anthony, Mark Backus, Dee and Larry Beck, Bill Bernat, Eliza Bethany, Michael Bloomberg, Mark Brady, Russell Brand, Howard Brooks, Tom Brown, Wanda Buckner, Bill Bungard, Ron Bush, Julia Cameron, Elise Campbell, Rachel Campbell, Jill Carlyle, Jane Carr-Kosanovich, Cate Caruth, Rebecca Castleton, Paul Clark, Lori Colbo, Darcelle XV/Walter Cole, Sue Cordes, Gary Craig, Vera Croce, Norrie Crockett, Michael Darcher, Jolee and Joseph Darnell, Anna David, Misha and Mike Davis, Clark Deem, Loretta Diehl, Patti Dobrowolski, Margi Domholt, Monique DuBose, Renata and George Dunkle, Jessica Dykstra, Michael Elliott, Erin Everett, Gwyn Fisher, Alina Frank, Judith Frost, Ingrid Garrido, Jo Anne Geron, George Goetschel,

Dale Golden, David Granirer, Peggy Grunwald, Rohit Gusain, David Hane, Johann Hari, Stephanus Adrian Hartanto, Denise Hartley, Heidi Henson, Suktipot Hinghoy, Donna Hitt, Lucinda Fabian Holder, Lyndsey Holder, Annie Holt, bell hooks, Darryl Inaba, Faiza Iqtadar, Dick Ireland, Allison Israel, Mary and Tom Johnson, Deborah Jordan, George Kao, Brian King, Stephen King, Donovan Kuehn, Anne Lamott, Diana LaRosa, Heidi Le, Anne Leahy, Laurel Lemke, Tom Link, Carol Chambers Lovelett, Nadia Rae Lubetski, Arthur Lubke, Polly MacLean, Leesa Madayag, Deb Malin, Tanya and Jim Manley, John O. Markham, Sandy Markham, Betty Marton, Gabor Mate, Johnny Mathis, Susan and Rona Matlow, Thomas McAvoy, Sherry McCreedy, Michael McDade, Bronwen McGarva, David McLellan, Alexandre Milagres, Ed Milan, Jackson Miller, Tim Miller, Shuna Morelli, Tulani Ncanywa, Barack and Michelle Obama, Lu O'Brien, Ricky Osborne, Jody Pilarski, Susan Pirnia, Joy Plies, Jaeynka Postupack, Thomas A. Power, Nancy Powers, Karen Ragan, Anthony and Claudia Rega, Michael Rega, Christopher Relken, Keith Richards, Susie Riley, Jim Roi, Ka(r)l Rogers, Stuart Alan Rose, Marshall Rosenberg, Marshall Rosensweet, Eric Ross, Marion Ruppert, Bailey Sammons, Tim Sample, Ivan

Sanchez, Elizabeth Scott, David Sedaris, Barbara Sher, Chris Sherman, Jen Sincero, Sonu Singh, Derek Sivers, Diann Sheldon, Abigail Shipley-Rega, Andrea Smith, Patrick Snow, Jackie Stearns, Steve Strom, Daimon Sweeney, Sajjad Tariq, Larry Tee, Ken Tomas, Angelia Trinidad, Laura Valdez, Jenny Van West, Ava Sweeney Vaughn, Walter Viers, Vanessa Spack Walker, Pip and Tammy Walter, Riley Waring, Dawn Warnaca, Randy Weled, Robert West, Robert A. (Bob) Whitney and Beth Whitney-Teeple, Melissa Wiese, Jeffrey Wigand, Jill Williams, Jessica Willis, Barbara Winter, and Hsushi Yeh.

Some of you helped save or transform my life; some helped make it worth saving. May your life be blessed as you have blessed others and mine.

NOTES

PREFACE

1. I'd also add, *If you want to have fun and do your best while you're going fast or slow, bring some friends along!*
2. https://www.patreon.com/user?u=21607045

INTRODUCTION

1. https://youtu.be/j4ZLb4afIJw
2. 12 Step fellowships and groups are mutual support organizations for the purpose of addressing addictions and other compulsions.

1. WORDS MATTER

1. Gabor Mate, a doctor, speaks of his compulsion to buy classical music, for goodness' sake! We each have our go-to's, to find comfort and alleviate pain.

7. SEE IT, SAY IT, DRAW IT, SHARE IT, DO IT (AND LET IT DO YOU)

1. Share it on https://www.patreon.com/kickbuttstakenames or on Instagram at https://www.instagram.com/niccitinafree or on Facebook at https://www.facebook.com/KickButtsTakeNames

12. TAP YOURSELF FREE

1. https://youtu.be/29KG8kA1_eM

13. COME OUT, COME OUT, WHEREVER YOU ARE

1. https://www.facebook.com/KickButtsTakeNames
2. https://www.instagram.com/niccitinafree
3. https://www.linkedin.com/in/joanna-niccitina-free-3568573/

14. NO MORE NICE DEAD PEOPLE

1. Nonviolent Communication: A Language of Life by Marshall Rosenberg

16. BETTER LIVING THROUGH BETTER CHEMISTRY (OR TO NICOTINE OR NOT TO NICOTINE)

1. And still are, based on the current research.
2. She was also decisively against vaping, even then, referring to vape devices as 'crack pipes.'

ABOUT THE AUTHOR

Joanna NicciTina Free is a dedicated smoker-turned-buttkicker obsessed with freedom of choice – yours and everyone else's. Whether writing books, putting "recruitment" cards in public ashtrays, doing standup comedy, tapping in a coffeehouse or conference, or walking in the streets and smoking areas dressed as a giant drag-inspired cigarette butt, it's All About Freedom, tobactivism (and fun).